Getting Out of a Stress Mess!

A Guide for Kids

Written by
Michaelene Mundy

Illustrated by
R. W. Alley

Abbey Press
St. Meinrad, IN 47577

For Emily, Patrick, and Michael,
who have shared many stress-free,
relaxing times with their Mom and Dad.
Thanks!

Published by One Caring Place
Abbey Press
St. Meinrad, Indiana 47577

Library of Congress Catalog Number
00-103689

ISBN 0-87029-348-6

Printed in the United States of America

A Message to Parents, Teachers, and Other Caring Adults

Adults often feel that kids "have it made." Compared to our complex and hectic lives, our children's lives seem care-free. But, in fact, children today don't have it as easy as we think—or as easy as we wish they had it.

Some of the stress children experience is a natural part of growing up. Every day they confront many new experiences and are expected to master new tasks and knowledge. Because so much that a child encounters is either a brand-new or rare occurrence, however, the child does not have "experience" to fall back on, as adults do.

Part of the stress that kids contend with today is cultural. In our society, we sometimes put pressure on children as we try to expose them to all the things we *think* they need. We don't want them to miss out on any sport or pastime or pursuit. We believe they need to excel in order to feel good about themselves. Yet the truth is that a child doesn't have to be on the all-star team, or win the spelling bee, or have the main part in the play, or have the neatest room in the neighborhood to be well-adjusted, healthy, and successful.

One way to take the pressure off kids is to encourage them to look at the positives in their lives—their good efforts and their successes, no matter how small. Adults can also help children to dream about being better at whatever they do—without feeling that the world will end if they don't succeed in the most perfect way.

Children do not always have the words or the understanding to say, "I'm feeling stressed." But the signs of stress will inevitably show up in their behavior. May this book help you to recognize a child who's feeling pressured, and guide him or her toward healthy, productive ways of turning a "stress mess" into "less stress."

—Michaelene Mundy

What Is Stress?

Stress is a feeling of being "under pressure"—sort of like a pot of water boiling on the stove. The pot actually shakes, and you can hear the lid rattle. Both adults and kids can get this kind of "pressured" feeling.

Stress usually happens when there's too much of something going on—like too many things changing at once...or too much noise...too much fighting...or too much homework.

Stress can also happen when there's *too little* of something—too little time to practice or to get to a game...not enough rest or quiet...or people thinking *you're too little* to be able to do things.

ELF HOLLOW
SPELLING BEE
JUDGE
JUDGE

What Does Stress Feel Like?

Stress can feel like worry. You may be afraid that you will disappoint your mom, dad, or coach unless you win the race or hit a home run. You might want to win a game or a contest so much that you feel very nervous.

Stress can also feel like sadness. You may be sad that something in your life is changing, but you can't do anything about it. Your stomach might hurt and you might even feel "shaky."

Different kids act in different ways when they are under stress. You may feel tired and slowed down, or nervous and restless. You might get in more fights with your brother or sister, or have trouble at school. Or you might feel like just being alone.

What Gives YOU Stress?

Do you feel stressed when people are watching you perform at school or at a sports event? Do you feel nervous because you want to do really well so your parents will be proud of you?

Kids can get stressed at times that might surprise you—happy times like Christmas, or on vacation, or during a weekend at Grandma's. Stress can happen at times like these because you get extra excited and because your daily routine is changed.

Feeling Stressed Without Knowing Why

If you could wish for anything in the world, what would it be? Your wish can give you a clue about what is making you feel stressed.

Maybe you wish that you never have to go to school again. Is that because there is something about school that's really hard for you? Your parents and teacher can help you figure out what's bothering you and how to make it easier for you.

10
10
10
11

Some Stress Is Normal

You cannot wave a magic wand and make stress go away forever, but you can learn how to handle it.

The first step is to know that it's okay to feel stress. You are not the only person who gets tense and nervous about things. Your friends do, too, and so do adults. Ask others what they do to help themselves relax.

It is also okay not to be perfect. Parents know it takes courage just to be on stage or step up to bat. They really mean it when they say they are proud of you just for trying. You don't have to be a star or hit a home run. No matter how you do, they will still love you.

2
1
3
E
2ND
1ST

Give Yourself a Break Today

If you're feeling stressed, it helps to relax. When you relax, you feel rested, peaceful, and comfortable.

Things that you enjoy doing are good ways to relax—maybe riding a bike, reading a book, or going for a walk. What makes you feel relaxed?

Think about what you would do if school were suddenly called off because of snow. Would you get out your construction set and build something? Ask someone to play a board game? Have popcorn and watch a movie? Rearrange your room? Why not do that relaxing, fun thing right now?

Express Your Stress!

It really helps to admit you are feeling stress and to talk with someone about it. You may be surprised how much better you feel just from saying, "I feel stressed!"

If you are worried about something coming up—like a test, big game, or trip to the doctor—tell a parent. Talk with someone who has been through this same kind of thing before and ask what to expect. The more you know, the less nervous you will be.

Express your stress to God, too. God wants to hear what's on your mind. You can talk to God about what is bothering you, no matter what it is. God loves you and wants to help your heart feel peaceful.

E

Too Much to Do?

It's great to have the chance to do sports and other activities. But if your free time is totally filled up with lessons, practices, or games, you don't have time to just "be a kid." You need "ME" time, when you can do what YOU want to do.

Your parents might think you enjoy all your activities, especially if you are trying hard to make them proud of you. But if you are feeling too busy, you should tell them.

Together you can talk about whether you need to cut back on your activities. You don't have to stop doing everything. Cutting back on just one thing may give you the time you need to relax.

Getting Your Balance

Stress is like being pushed and pulled in different directions. It can make you "lose your balance."

Eating healthy food and getting exercise every day helps you to keep your balance. If you live near a park or woods, spend some time outdoors in nature. This is a great way to get rid of stress.

Getting enough rest is important, too. When you are tired, you may feel anxious about something that wouldn't normally bother you. After a good sleep, you might just wake up and realize you're not feeling stressed out anymore.

Family Stress

Stress can be "catching." If a parent or brother or sister is under a lot of stress, you will probably know it. And that may make you feel stressed, too, because you can sense that something is wrong.

Try saying to that person, "You seem stressed out. Can I do anything to help you relax?" Being relaxed can be catching, too!

With families so busy these days, they sometimes don't get enough time to relax together. Talk to your parents about making one night each week "Family Night," when you can all spend time together having fun.

PAY THIS NOW!
INVOICE
BILL

Report on Volcanos
MARCH
Step 1: Go to library
2: Get supplies
3: write report
4 Build Volcano
5 practice report

Getting Out of a Stress Mess

Sometimes our imaginations make us think things are much worse than they really are. Instead of worrying about homework or studying for a test, just do it! Don't wait till the last minute to start. If you do a little bit at a time, it's much less stressful.

When you have a lot of things you need to do, you might be afraid you'll forget some of them. Making a list can help.

You'll see that you don't have a MILLION things to do—just five, or eight, or twelve. Making a list also helps you to think about what is really important and what is not. And it reminds you to do those important things.

TABLE
17
VOLCANO PROJECT
Judge
JUDGE
JUDGE
JUDGE
JUDGE
JUDGE

When You Have to Do Something Stressful...

Take a deep breath and let it out slowly. In your imagination, picture yourself doing okay.

Then take your turn—at bat, spelling a word, or whatever it is you have to do. Whether you "win" or not, you will feel relief that the scary part is over. And, remember, you "win" every time you try, not just when you get "first place." If things didn't turn out the way you wanted, that doesn't mean it's going to happen that way *every* time—or even the next time.

Notice how you feel afterward—happy, relaxed, relieved. The next time your turn comes, tell yourself: "I did it before and I can do it again!"

Be Silly!

Laughing is a great way to relax. What makes you laugh? Being silly? Knock-knock jokes? Standing on your head?

Do you have a dog, cat, fish, or lizard? Watch how your pet relaxes. Pets know how just to be themselves—instead of being too busy or in a hurry. Let your pet teach you how to relax!

If you are having trouble going to sleep at night because you are feeling too stressed out, think of the silliest thing that happened to you that day. It will make you smile and take your mind off your worries.

Less Stress—More Joy!

As a human being, you are always going to have some stress. Every year, there is a first day of school. There are teachers, tests, homework, speeches, lessons, and games. There will always be changes in your life and things that are new to you.

But as you find out more about what gives you stress and what helps you relax, you will grow stronger and smarter about stress. You will be able to guess when stress is going to hit and take steps to handle it.

And with less stress, you will feel freer to enjoy life and just be a kid!

Michaelene Mundy holds degrees in elementary education, as well as graduate degrees in school and community counseling. She has taught third and fourth graders, worked with learning-disabled children, and has served as a counselor on the college level. The mother of three children, she now works as a high school guidance counselor. Michaelene Mundy has written two previous titles in the Elf-help for Kids book series, *Sad Isn't Bad* and *Mad Isn't Bad*.

R. W. Alley is the illustrator for the popular Abbey Press adult series of Elf-help books, as well as an illustrator and writer of children's books. He lives in Barrington, Rhode Island, with his wife, daughter, and son.